Dark Recesses of the Heart

Dark Recesses of the Heart

Poems on Love, Brooding, and Mental Health

Isaac Kight

Isaac Kight

CONTENTS

First Printing, 2023

Mild Yellow

Introduction

Introduction

Setting out to write a second book of poetry is a much different process from the first. I have a much better idea how to format my work. It simplifies the process from an organizational point of view. My priorities, feelings, and inspiration have also changed betwixt books. This affords the reader of this book of poetry a relatively unique experience relative to the previous. Dark Recesses of the Mind took the reader through my expressions as I began treatment for terrible childhood traumas. The path to healing from severe PTSD began with intensely negative thoughts and feelings.

There were positive themes in that book as well: love, mentorship, beauty, and even flirtation with sexual expression. In the time since the publishing of the first book I have continued to have the muse but now that I have gone through the process of beginning treatment and entered the exploration of my own feelings and character, I have different sensations to express.

I have written more on feelings about the world and myself. Explored beauty, love, self-disdain, and self-love. In the last book I wrote an introduction that explained my favorite poets who inspired me in their style and described my experimentation with poetic structures and concepts. In this introduction I need simply say, I have added a few new influences but mostly continued in a similar vein, but with a different set of intense feelings to express.

When I have posted my poetry publicly on social media in the past, others have expressed that they feel similar sensations, especially depression, and that they found healing in knowing that they were not alone. It is my hope that this work enriches the reader, describes relating pain to those who suffer, conveys the pangs of suffering to those who have happier lives (and can thus better appreciate that happiness), and generally offers a vulnerability I feel uncomfortable with in interpersonal interactions.

Longing

Model: Eleanore Dystopia

I

Featured Poems

The Longing

Do you long for my touch?
Feelings strong for me as such
As much as I long to feel you
That I might die to be born anew

When you gaze into my own eyes
Is it with love's daze and all its ties?
Do you desire so to be at my side?
A feeling higher than you can abide

Do you feel for me and do I
For you to seal my love in the sky?
When I am afar do you ache?
Wishing upon a star for my sake

If but my fingers could gently slide
My hand lingers, I fear to confide
Down the slope of your neck so elegant
We could elope a matter so delicate

If for my caress you too fantasize
This love we'll harness ever to tantalize
These two made one by lofty passion
Torn 'sunder by none as a life they fashion

The Poet's Heart

I could not keep my feelings behind bars
The poet's heart is covered in deep scars
We live in a world so cruel and colorless
The shape and form of my distress

My anger flashes hot like lightening
With primordial intensity so frightening
If only my fists could strike and kill
Oh what a high, such a thrill

Yet the allure of violence is terrifying
Its indecency not at all mystifying
For me it is not a viable solution
For my deep pain's subtle dilution

For my plight there can be no justice
Human evils so vast and venomous
Abused, beaten, enveloped, and beset
The damage of my illness I cannot reset

I came to the world with love and treasure
To impart kindness in copious measure
From the start I knew right from wrong
Only to play out life's miserable song

Oh divine and mighty king!
Why to me did you do this thing?!
For I was born in the valley of death's shadow
As my goodness shown so brightly aglow

Not even in ignorant bliss could I take comfort
You gave me a mind and will not to distort
Where are the green pastures to be found?
My cup runs dry, troubles do so abound

How I long to transcend this suffering
If just a moment's peace it could bring
All is one, the other is but a mirror
To hurt the other hurts the self so clear

How many have enjoyed hurting me?
Perverse pleasure they did see
I do not seek to hurt them back
What good would it do me to attack?

Here alone, empty, and distressed
By mankind I am unimpressed
My energy could have been such a blessing
But their torments merely left me stressing

Now I see life's sadistic nature
With its cruel nomenclature
I feel the pangs of my tortured past
My scarred heart is ready to beat its last

Nirvana

Kiss upon her neck
Caress along her arm gently
The sweet taste of her red lips

The passion of life
My one true love in my arms
She is bliss, pure Nirvana

A Sedoka is a form of Waka (Japanese) poetry consisting of two stanzas of 5-7-7 syllable non-rhyming verse.

Nirvana

Photo by: Dani Oliver
Model: Mariia Zubtsova
Model requests charity to
Help2Ukraine.org

Kind Soul

There is born once in a while
A soul kind and gentle with style
A deep thinker with intense feeling
Art pours forth from his lips seething

Yet this world is not for his kind
Cruelty and banality do bind
In a world cold, colorless, and cruel
He brings light but plays the fool

Flowers and beauty he brings to the fore
To show them another way to explore
A life of pleasure and happiness can be
If only everyone would set themselves free

The ties that bind and make most blind
Can be broken with love if we find
The will to express ourselves without limits
Sharing our pure feeling with our intimates

The world strikes back in a rush
His passion does it seek to crush
They poke, pry, and stoke his pain
To imbue him with fiery self-disdain

In this dark place must he struggle
As his thoughts they try to befuddle
Yet does he not grow thick skinned
He remains vulnerable against the wind

By society is he ripped and torn
They make him wish he'd not been born
G-d sends kind souls so all can see
True strength and what it means to be free

The End

Will this miserable life ever end?
Negative feelings from which I cannot fend
Swirling emotions how they mix and blend
Into dark recesses they do send

A smiling face, calm demeanor I pretend
The pain rends my heart, it will not mend
Snarling, twisting my life does it bend
There is no hope, no help to lend

Intertwining through my soul it does wend
What I might give for one true friend
To life's whims does my path commend
On misery's spite does my pleasure depend

But that my course I could amend
A bright new chapter I would then append
With my demons I must quickly contend
All my emotions I now quietly expend

A new perspective does abruptly apprehend
This pensive time perhaps I misspend…?
This suffering I might somehow transcend?
Alas, perhaps my own heart I offend

That is not at all anything I might intend
My own feelings I do constantly distend
To my soul I do often condescend
It pays me naught, there is no dividend

Suppose, a greater power does superintend?
Giving life as a precious gift, a g-dsend
The futility of suffering on I comprehend
To my final affairs I must diligently attend

II

Love Poems

Wanted

I wanted to take her hand
I was afraid, you understand?
It was dark and we were alone
It would reassure the scare prone

I think she wanted me to
To do what I was scared to do
Only one way to know for sure
My hand did not reach or stir

We walked, laughed, and strayed
In that moment I might have stayed
Alas time ran short, our walk ended
From love's embrace I had fended

A hug good night the time was right
I could not muster the strength as I might
So we parted without our due
Was she disheartened too?

Feelings are another way of talking
Emotions flowing as we were walking
What were we saying with our hearts
I may never know, I failed for starts

Disbelief

I do not believe in Apophis and his chaos
Dionysus and Mythras are to me but dross
I do not believe in Earth-shattering apotheosis
The end of civilizations just putrid necrosis
I do not believe the promises of the political
I find their transparent lies so antithetical
I do not believe in the institutions of men
Their incompetence and devastation so Zen
I do not believe in the words of false prophets
Their lies emptiness, naught in their tenets
I do not believe in pseudo-science so lame
Their false predictions are wrong all the same
I do not believe in power and strength
They all fail me eventually, weakness at length
I do not believe in modern medicine
Or that the light bulb was invented by Edison
I do not believe in the value of gold
Or shiny metals polished and bold

I believe in the power of my love
A passion for my cherished dove
For you are the light that brightens the Heavens
As my affection perpetually leavens
I believe you are the one
Who shines on me like the sun
I believe we were meant to be
Take my hand and we shall see

I believe we will have a grand adventure
Even if at times it will mean my censure
I believe that so long as I have you
I am fortunate that you love me too

Valkyrie

Valkyrie on a Pegasus

The Valkyrie

Lovely Valkyrie carry me off to Frejya's field
There upon the grass, I'll make you yield
In Valhalla's halls our love be sealed
As before me 'twas you who kneeled

Eternal beauty with long golden hair
Let me play upon you if you dare
Into your loving eyes I shall stare
Viking and Valkyrie an undefeatable pair

Many a foe felled by my sharp blade
As I conquered, my ambition bade
My thoughts of you ne'er did fade
I must be carried off by a lovely maid

Alas in battle did I finally meet my end
As against my enemies I did fend
My prayer into the sky did I send
To Asgard my soul doth lend

From the sky she rode with a scream
At first I feared 'twas but a dream
A blond beauty upon her stead so cream
Her armor did so glisten and gleam

Lovely Eir, she came to spirit me away
For I had been cleaved on that dark day
Yet, I died sword in hand, it is the way
Thus, soon with my Valkyrie in a field I lay

Most great men with this be sated
Brought to Valhalla who would not be elated?
Yet, for I 'twas not my repast to be fated
Until with this alluring Valkyrie I was mated

How Bless'd I Am

This love so grand a woman join'd to me
Her hair of mink, her eyes of axinite
Her gentle shoulders white like snow I see
Her lips are fiery a passion held in sight

Her disp'sition is bright and blue as sky
So lovely, lively, bright a fine young lass
If only with me she might then dare to lie
Her form does flow and curve so smooth as glass

Her brilliant mind is mine I will not share
Her sharp and awesome intellect does shine
No offense I would give to her nor dare
This queenly grand sweet nymph a love of mine

How I do long for her all my dear life
How bless'd am I dear Rachel is my wife

III

Japanese Waka Poetry

Japanese Waka Poetry

Japanese Waka poetry centers on lines of verse based on how many syllables are contained in each line. This is typically non-rhyming. The cryptic nature of such poetry, especially when composed in English has always enticed me. Many are familiar with the Haiku which is a poem constructed of three lines: the first of 5 syllables, then 7 syllables, and a final line of 5 syllables. This is a shorter version of the preceding form the Katauta, which is composed of three lines of 5-7-7 syllables. My favorite form is the Sedoka which is made up of two Katautas, or two 5-7-7 stanzas. The Haikus for this edition are below, followed by the Sedokas.

秋

Autumn

Haikus

Pink Blossom

The first pink blossom
Spring will be upon us soon
Beauty unbounded

Fate

Pink cherry blossom
She knows nothing of her fate
Her petals will fall

Autumn

The leaves are turning
Red, rust, and yellow colors
The sunset season

Outcast

Painted by Dian Petrov

Sedokas

Outcast

So inadequate
Too awkward for this cruel world
Unwelcome is my presence

I don't belong here
Nor there nor anywhere I go
Very lonely is the outcast

White Rose

Isaac Kight Original Art

Beyond Expectation

So transitory
The beauty of a flower
Unmatched is the white rose

Purity of form
Without blemish, fault, or care
Beyond all expectation

A Tyrant in the Fold

A wolf in the fold
Hidden among all the sheep
He laughs that they see him not

A tyrant in view
We all know just what he is
Still, we do not challenge him

Cherished

When you are so far
I long to be by your side
I cherish you above all

I feel your longing
I need to have you near me
How I so wish to hold you

Cherished

Model: Eleanore Dystopia

Truth of Death

What lies beyond life?
Many are curious
For them life remains vibrant

No questions have I
For I am already dead
Depression has taught me truth

Courtesy Licensable

Suddenly Taken

I was so tempted
A happy future was seen
Possibilities endless

Suddenly taken
Ripped away by the wind
My misery unending

Cherry Blossom

Isaac Kight Original Art

Passion Anew

Light gust of warm breeze
The orchids are now in bloom
Cherry blossoms flutter and fall

A sparkle of youth
In her eyes so lovingly
Our passion now stirs anew

Model: Eleanore Dystopia

Passion

On the horizon
My heart burns so delightful
The eternal pain descends

It is my great love
She is love springing all time
Passion wells only for her

Agony

A life of great pain
Torment from the beginning
Building intense agony

I must suffer on
My mission is incomplete
The blossom will slowly wilt

Agony

Isaac Kight Original Art

IV

Feelings and Other Topics

Heart Scratch

I am told I don't form attachments
Appropriate emotional entanglements
For this I am called one who is disordered
Because my heart is guarded and bordered

PTSD they call it and severe mental illness
The noise of humanity, how I long for stillness
I prefer to be with my thoughts alone
With others I am awkward and injury prone

For some have I ventured to love and care
Only to be hurt and insulted if I dare
Even those who do not intend harm
Disappoint and fall short without charm

Yet, it is I who is disordered and broken
In others I seek not comfort, even a token
With humanity I am frequently distraught
For most I can care but little or naught

People commit such inhuman crimes
We live in chaotic and destructive times
Why should I have faith in others?
When their disapproval but smothers

I have little in common, I do not relate
I do not belong, my words cannot sate
I exhaust myself and it bears no fruit
I try my hardest, but it will not suit

Given the failings and faults of mankind
To which we are expected to be blind
Why is it I who is regarded as faulty?
In a world of people bitter and salty

Is it really me that is the problem here?
I am miserable because of all I hold dear
Perhaps there is blame to go around
The behavior of others is often unsound

Still it is I who does eternally suffer
Distance to others a safe buffer
If there are but few to whom you attach
Upon the heart less injury does scratch

Heart Scratch

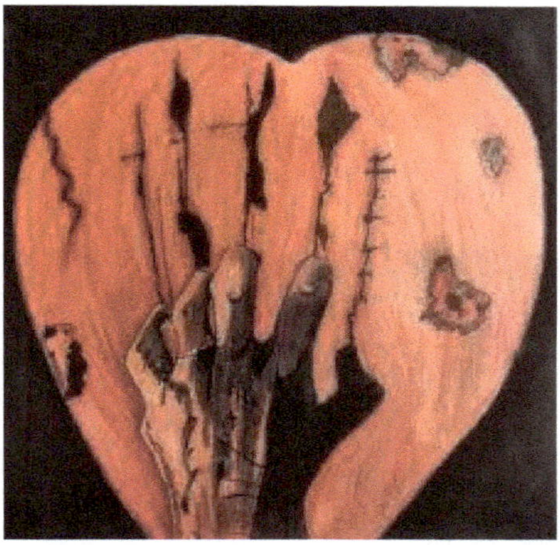

Courtesy The Scratched Heart
Facebook Page

Oneness

Painted by Rob Gonsalves

Oneness

Head on the pillow I drifted off to sleep
Into my subconscious, a dream so deep
In wisps and mist, off to a distant realm
My vast mind no longer at the helm

Suddenly I stood at death's door
As my body lay up on the floor
My heart beat for the very last time
It was the end, I heard the chime

Whisked away down the river's course
As I melted into creation's source
At that moment I was no longer me
Drop into the ocean, I was part of the sea

In that instant, I begin to understand
All that exists is in "His" hand
I could perceive it all from strings to stars
I knew everything from quarks to blazars

Feeling all alive from eukaryote to sentient
We knew all things beyond the nescient
I was cognizant that I had always been one
With all things since creation had begun

When we do harm to any other
It is also ourselves whom we smother
So many wisemen tried to teach this
Many great lessons, yet we go so amiss

Kohelet, Spinoza, Zeno, Buddha, and Lao Tzu
How was this ignored by all of you?
From the dawn of life, I was met with strife
Beaten and abused with insults rife

Shunned and hated, treated always as less
A life of dread and loneliness, I must confess
All those who treated me with such distain
We're also causing themselves great pain

At oneness with all, I know I was not alone
Among millions of species, the abuse prone
I had also caused a little harm as well
I did not grasp until enlightenment's knell

Most of my life I strived to be kind
Moral discipline among the blind
Now rejoined to all, my efforts lauded
The efforts of the decent roundly applauded

No longer me, many particles in the sea
Mixed with everything now, past, and to be
Wrapped in the warmth of universality
Freed from limited, human temporality

From the clanging of an alarm, I did wake
Ripped from Nirvana for consciousness' sake
Losing so much of what I had been aware
Returned to this life's eternal nightmare

Fastened to the dream, I tried to recall
What it was like to perceive it all
Condemned to this life, I must explore
Until I breathe nevermore, nevermore

Feelings

Why do we have these accursed emotions?
Anger, fear, sadness, and loving devotions?
A primitive mechanism for interaction
Animalistic feelings for seeing infraction

When one forms attachment to another
It is pure torture, my will to smother
I reach out with feeling to relate
An unnamed inner want to sate

Frequently rebuffed, ridiculed, and shunned
Human cruelty leaves me often stunned
Why is there so little love and kindness?
Too much hate and willful blindness

I cannot be vulnerable to be attacked
In my childhood, pain this did attract
My outer critic rages by others unheard
Against those with my affections undeterred

My inner critic attacks me too!
"Keep amoral company, you do!"
Bullied within and without by forces unseen
Internalized where confidence should have been

I have made a few friends in my time
Most are good people in their prime
Yet so often I find others less than ideal
In some cases, detestable for real!

There are those unable to be moral
Who are easily misled by lies oral
When they cross that inviolable line
From their presence I must resign

By the affront I am incurably offended
The arm of my moral flexibility distended
Somehow, it is always me at fault
When others do morality assault

This dilemma much anxiety does cause
I battle fear and inward bullies without pause
I do not know the solution to my query
Deep within me my feelings I must burry

Is that right? The correct answer?
As this eats at me like terminal cancer?
I do not know which way to turn
Myself or the other I must spurn

It is I, myself whom I most detest
All pleasures from him I must divest
Moral boundaries are for those with value
Needs of the detestable ignore shall you?

If only these emotions I did not possess
My happiness so often they do repress
To be purely logical, detached from humanity
Would be such a great blessing, a commodity

Parting Ways

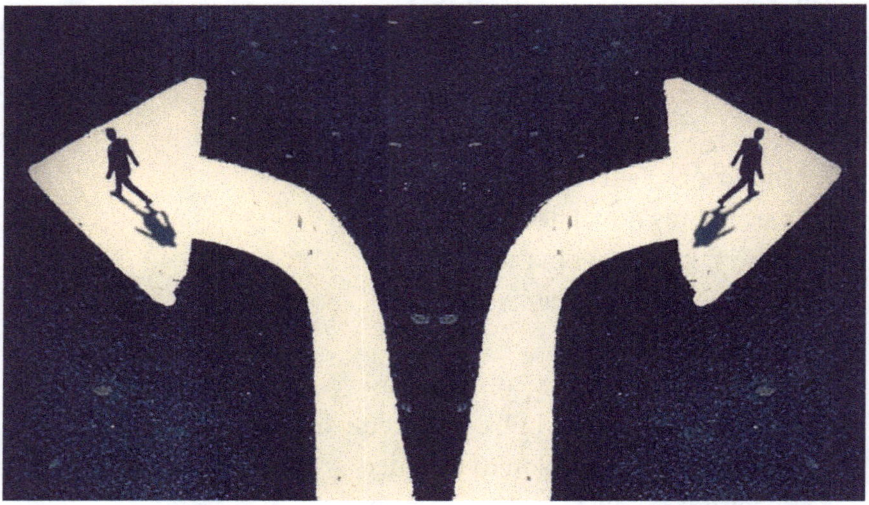

Courtesy Licensable

Parting Ways

A distance between what is real
And that which I truly feel
A chasm between you and I
That I simply cannot deny

Set on a separate trajectory
As light through a refractory
No longer close but growing far
Soon to be as a remote star

It cannot be by us denied
That this friendship tried
No longer seems to suit
It has born a bitter fruit

I go on my path perpendicular
Divergent brushes of the calligrapher
It was rewarding in its time
Now it's end does urgently chime

The bonds burned we go our ways
But in memory it kindly stays
I wish you well on your journey
I hope your path is not too thorny

Unwhole

Alone in social isolation
Utter emotional desolation
Disappointed again and again
How it drives me insane!

It is proof, it must be true
I'm not a real person to you
Or to anyone it seems
Though my heart beams

Where ever do I belong?
Is there a crowd singing my song?
Time with others free of anxiety
The intense pain never in paucity

I suppose I am extraverted
But social failure is oft asserted
Alone in a small crowd
Truths I dare not speak aloud

As usual it is me, myself, and I
A lonely show until I die
I know not why I try, why begin?
Among others I will never fit in

Kolinahr

Most of my life I avoided my feelings
Persistent suffering, emotional bleedings
Irrational and illogical they are to me
If but wholly rational I could always be

These feelings are a curse I want them not
Love, affection, and desire a disease caught
Hate, anger, to despise feel empowering
To those who in fear are ever cowering

Yet to feel these must I ever constantly
Feel panic, anxiety, and despair presently
Depression always haunts my days
How it tortures me in so many ways

If only I could undergo the Kolinahr
To purge all emotion going so far
Then a proper Vulcan would I be
Never again this suffering would I see

To be human is to be cursed completely
Mental illness haunts us all so neatly
Those of us who were born unwanted
Ever to be beaten, spat upon, and taunted

We have no value, there is no worth
We are cast aside to be another's mirth
Sadly, I cannot purge these feelings
They must always harass my dealings

If only there was a path to pure logic
Away from these emotions so vitriolic
Unfortunately, this path to us is closed
The only other path, the question posed?

There is only one way to escape the curse
To breathe no more carried away in a hearse

Grand Tetons

Oh! Grand Tetons standing so proud
In the quiet breeze thou art so loud
What great aspirations and hopes
Have climbed so loftily upon your slopes?

Exquisite formations blissfully at play
In the stones which upon you lay
How many played and hunted in your soot?
Among the Shoshone, Crow, and Blackfoot

Driving men to pursue great feats
By your beautiful, rocky teats
Great monuments of igneous stone
Inspiration to the adventure prone

Grand Tetons Mountain Peaks
Isaac Kight Original Art

Connections

Surrounded by others I feel so alone
Socially awkward and accident prone
My heart so numb I feel so cold
I am very tired, I feel so old

I want to feel a connection to others
Like I belong among my brothers
Yet every bond is a vulnerability so frail
Their actions can easily injure and impale

The borders of my soul are so weak
My outlook on friendship is quite bleak
To form attachments with others I abhor
So easily hurt by those whom I adore

I find that I still need friends
Though it doesn't suit my ends
Trapped in impossible contradiction
So in keeping with my life's direction

What now is my path to be?
How many friends shall I see?
From the many I'll need to hew
Down to the minimal, necessary few

Cycle of Life

When we are born from the top
The ethereal ocean becomes the drop
When we die it is the right notion
That the drop becomes the ocean

It is the natural order of this life
Begun in screaming youthful strife
We grow and the basics we do learn
Slowly into to adolescents we turn

With energy and passion we begin
To stand on our own not forsaken
As men and women we build our lives
As for a better life each constantly strives

New life is born the fruit of love
Giving life a blessing from above
We guide our children to do right
And protect from evil in our sight

We work and struggle to secure
A future for our offspring to ensure
We age and tire in our enterprise
All too soon our old age we realize

Eventually the end time arrives
A final resting no one survives
A life lived to its very best
As we are finally laid to rest

Belonging

I want so desperately to belong
Almost every social situation feels wrong
I do not fit wherever I go, in the throng
My bond with others is never strong

Why do I bother and try to fit in?
I am not a real person but made of tin
I have no heart, no feelings akin
I never feel comfortable in my own skin

Why do I live isolated so?
No other way can I know
There is no other path to go
Hope to belong only brings me low

No matter how hard others try
To include me, their efforts to pry
I still feel an outcast, I am a lie
At times I sit alone just to cry

In the end I am eternally alone
The seeds of my exclusion sown
From everyone I've ever known
I can only sigh to myself and bemoan

This is the pattern so well rehearsed
I fit for a time, but only at first
My eccentric personality then does burst
In social matters I am truly cursed

Feigning Life

Courtesy Licensable

Feigning Life

It is that season once more
That cuts deeply into my core
When depression arrives surreal
I no longer know if my life is real

Each day I go through the motions
Satisfying other's complex notions
That I am alive at my regular task
I smile and go on, but beneath the mask

I am just pretending to be alive?
As to meet my quotas I strive
Have I died? Is this all illusion?
One giant abstract delusion?

My feelings flood as if to burst
But then they ebb, am I cursed?
I was not a real person at beginning
In life's first torturous inning

So it infinitely endless, on and on
As new torments often spawn
Why must I keep up this pretense?
I am not alive, it makes no sense!

Neither am I truly at my expiry
No blaze of death, hot and fiery
So I am trapped between tick and tock
Not quite alive nor dead

Disappointment

Disappointment is my lot
Why this is, I know not
I struggle so hard to rise
Just to meet my dream's demise

What I am today is quite less
Than I should be when at my best
Tell me why I feel so low
I certainly do not know

How can I my best reach?
These insurmountable walls breach
If it were simple as a leap
I'd still find the effort too steep

No Guarantees

Are those fries covered in chili-cheese?
Oh yes, I'd love to have some please!
The aroma wafting is so much a tease
I know too many will bring heart disease

So delicious my anxiety to ease
Just this once the chance I'll seize
And some ice cream my tongue to freeze
I'll try new flavors of sweet teas

See the pollen from the bees
Fall through the air in the breeze
Though it might make me sneeze
The awe brings me to me knees

I'll get in the car, grab the keys
From life's troubles everyone flees
The wanton and corrupt sleaze
We have no choice but to pay the fees

The fruit of life I want to squeeze
Even when everyone else disagrees
Pleasures and pains off come in threes
Most people at least try to appease

When the truth comes from the appointees
Made fair by self-important referees
My mind ponders, considers, and foresees
The numerous facets in their degrees

I know this wordplay is like a trapeze
It will annoy the powerful in their liveries
They are not the intended addressees
You should know there are no guarantees

V

Depression Poems

Depression's Slave

Emotions are ever my life's bane
They drive me to misery so inane
For but few moments of pleasure
Intense anxiety in unequal measure

Those brief times when I feel not so bad
The few happiest moments I've ever had
Caused me such inescapable pain
Now I must make the matter plain

Oh to be a fictitious Vulcan!
Years of evenness rarely broken
To have ever an even keel
Nothing too intense to feel

Then of this curse I'd be free
Free to pursue what's best for me
How I sacrifice a few moments of bliss
And even love's one true kiss

I give it all up not to suffer so
Without hesitation, I'd do it though
I am depression's most humble slave
A rare moment of pleasure cannot save

Rustic

Isaac Kight Original Art

To Remain Alive

All my life I have struggled to survive
This deadly illness forced upon me
A constant battle just to be alive
The illness will not allow me to be

I cannot prosper if all I do is get by
Yet scraping by is the most I can do
The pressure builds as to work I try
I have suffered so, no one has a clue

Dealing with others I so terribly fear
Everyone mocks me, I am put down
My very heart does it so deeply sear
Only trepidation I feel, like a clown

So many rely upon my support
I must succeed in my enterprise
My feelings twist, warp, and contort
As kind words prove to be only lies

This life I did not truly want
Few understand the effort I make
Only to hear another's cruel taunt
With sadness to each new day I wake

It is too difficult for me, I cannot win
No matter what I do to advance
My actions are drowned out in the din
I look on the injustice of life askance

Each day I rise above that pain
Step into the sun and strive
Two steps forward, one back slow gain
This is my conflict to remain alive

Nature of Humanity

Why was I born a human being?
All this evil and cruelty I am seeing
An ignorant species without distinction
If ever there was a being worthy of extinction

I did not want this life for me
Ever present pain and misery
I cannot be calm, confident, or happy
I can barely love or be sappy

The fleet of my ills now compounded
Why I go on has me astounded
How I wish I could escape this illness
Attain quietly to the cool stillness

There is no cure and no relief
For my frequent, dolorous grief
Peace of mind is out of sight
Fear and anxiety oft put me to flight

Abuser, injured, and cast aside
My treatment I cannot abide
Yet am I not a monster enraged
Convict, Addict morality disengaged

This is strong evidence empirical
That I am in fact a walking miracle
Yet this life hurts too intensely
I want it over so immensely

Oh to love and be loved of fondness
There is far too little human kindness
Small waves of decency ripple
Reflecting off of others triple

If in a world in which I could thrive
It would be worth to pain to be alive
The suffering will end one glorious day
When this life finally slips away

Ballad of the Broken

I am utterly broken, I cannot be fixed
The pain will end only when I am deep sixed
If only the traumatic cause could be nixed
I work for healing results are mixed

I've happily taken sound advice
Yet my efforts do not suffice
Throughout my person does pain splice
I want to be well, that would be nice

Success Impossible

I must have all of the answers
I must cure all of the cancers
I must provide for those in need
With the fruit of my labors I do feed

Yet I cannot earn enough
Always short in life's cruel rebuff
Everything is set against me
I cannot be allowed simply to be

Why do I live when I am so useless?
Why work so hard for a result so baseless?
I cannot win no matter how hard I try
I push myself to the edge, soon I'll die

The pressure is far to much to bear
For my charges I do so care
I just want a little success
Some small effort of mine to bless

In the end it is all for naught
With constant failure is my life fraught
There is no meaning, no higher purpose
Just my torpor, the miserable corpus

Why cannot this life just end?
No more to provide and fend?
I have not the strength to go on
My armor is pierced, nothing more to don

Beaten, broken, upon jagged shoals
My life bereft of achieved goals
In the final calculus of my life's sum
A negative value, my feelings numb

Why did I continue this life to undertake
Knowing I would fail, given what is at stake
Still I suffered on against fate so merciless
Toward an end to completely pitiless

I did not want this life from the beginning
Especially knowing I would not be winning
I could have brought an end in years past
When less suffering my death would cast

I missed that chance for lack of gall
I struck out, I could not hit the ball
Now I must suffer on and do the impossible
Even though success is implausible

Success Impossible

Isaac Kight Original Art

Terminal Depression

For brief moments hope has infrequently flickered.
In this awful life foisted on me by the cruel universe.
Through these miserable times as with others I bickered.
Their words so often cold and terse.

I am at a loss, I know not how to go on.
Everything I touch I destroy, everyone I reach I harm.
I am nothing but a waste of material, failure's spawn.
Born devoid of that very human quality, without charm.

I have struggled against this monster insurmountable.
I have fought to bring basic success to this life.
I must give in to the what is inevitable.
I must surrender to the mercy of the knife.

There are those who have cared and tried the disease to wipe.
It is incurable, unstoppable, it is terminal.
I belong in the compost pile with the rest of the tripe.
I was a bad idea from the time germinal.

How I long for the end of this accursed experience!
If that I could command this damnable heart to cease!
I will give up my struggle and embrace mere dalliance.
Perhaps in total failure and listlessness there is peace.

Oh how the dead are enviable...

My Station

Courtesy Licensable

My Station

Born into a hopeless situation
Abuse and suffering my life's station
Thereafter little more than a pariah
A moralizing outcast like Jeremiah

It has been ever my loathsome lot
To be attacked by every cruel plot
No one cared for my frail feelings
I could be mistreated in all dealings

Even now looked upon with great suspicion
Everyone seeking my pending excision
Could I receive one simple kindness?
Amidst mankind's moral blindness

Each day the pain grows so intense
The hurdles I overcome so immense
Few perceive, let alone comprehend
The agony and anguish I must mend

Will these deep wounds never heal?
As I slowly learn how to feel
Forever cursed with mental injury
Eternally damned to functional disability

Given the many reasons afore listed
It is evident I should never have existed
After all the evils I had to survive
It is a miracle I am still alive

What will be my next verse?
A happy ending I might rehearse...?
If only an end to this torturous malady
Alas, only with my last breath's finality

Shadoe

In the dark shadow of his feeling
Cold and alone his life was peeling
Alone in the crowd so far from reality
Consumed by his own petty mortality

Somewhere on the path he was lost
He wandered aimlessly at great cost
Suffering in silence so palpable
Losing sight of that which is invaluable

Feigning a smile, a mild joke
As terrible sadness and pain did choke
A pal to others, a teacher and mentor
As he fought his internal tormentor

Eventually the misery reached fever pitch
A vision of the future he could not stitch
Escape from the strife he so sought
To an early end was he brought

Though he suffers this pain no more
He has left those who lov'd him sore
In our grief we will always insist
For all our lives he will be missed...

A poem in honor of Shadoe, a kind person lost to the illness of depression.

Shards

My life is crumbling into shards
The collapse of my house of cards
I feel the walls closing in fast
The pressure intense, I cannot last

Twisted Perception

Isaac Kight Original Art

Fading Strength

Blood flee from my veins
Free me from all my banes
The world is cold and cruel
Tortured like a hopeless fool

Comedy of my life please end
Out of this hateful world to send
Pain of my illness now spared
I tried to live, I truly dared

Suffering so intense I feel
No pleasure from my meal
Pulsing pressure in my core
I cannot stand it anymore

My departure would be the cause
Of so much suffering I pause
But I can no longer endure
My strength fades, my stamina poor

I do not know why it was me
Upon whom visited great misery
I know only that I am out of steam
Time to go it would seem

Over One Tree Hill

Isaac Kight Original Art

The Haze

My mind is full of the haze
Anxiety clouds my days
My consciousness will sink
I do not know, cannot think

Brought down from lofty height
My higher mind out of sight
Deep ideas now seem so vague
This illness is certainly a plague

Clear the haze, restore my brain
Before I am driven utterly insane
A great mind suddenly brought low
Anxiety is what trauma does sow

Stunted

My whole life by my illness consumed
My success dead, not to be exhumed
I cannot be what I wanted to be
I cannot enjoy what I wanted to see

The theft of my life by forces beyond
For simple health I have so fawned
A say, agency I have very little
Treated always like so much spittle

Why am I such a detestable thing?
Insults toward me does everyone fling
Cast down, forgotten, excluded, shunned
Yet by my capacity are so many stunned

An intellect sprawling, full of potential
Gifts so powerful, perhaps providential
Imagination without limits I find
Very few like me, of my kind

There is no place for me, no niche
My wants and dreams ever on a leash
What is a life with only half my due?
Do you feel this hamstrung too?

Why must greatness be so crushed?
Expression hampered and hushed
All I have ever wanted was my day to shine
Thanks to PTSD, this day will never be mine

A lifetime of pain from childhood abuse
There is no cure, it is of no use
From the world only kindness can I beg
Patience for this unshapely square peg

In youth, death nearly visited me often
My heart of stone, not easy to soften
All that is left, is to keep up the struggle
Small successes I desperately smuggle

Incomplete

As a person I am incomplete
Of missing parts I am replete
Un-nurtured and unloved in childhood
Protected as best one could

My emotional puzzle missing pieces
Demons in my mind life-long leases
Unable to love myself at all
Upon no self-comfort can I call

Difficulty I have in attaching to others
Either detached or my feeling smothers
Derided and shunned by cruel society
A sad tune played on life's calliope

As an adult I must fill the spaces
Fixing problems at all their paces
Mother's love was not there
No love for self can I spare

Father's protection I did posses
Insufficient against my distress
It is best when things are done right
A life of suffering seems my plight

Failure's Return

After months of anxiety and more
Now this depression I abhor
Once again on the precipice I stand
Ultimate failure in my very hand

It goes this way every time I try
Success for a time, then I fry
Mental illness again brings me down
The morass of anguish, I slowly drown

"Once more unto the breach, dear friends..."
As into the abyss my mood descends
No longer alive, just a shell
Not yet dead, a living hell

Failure again rears it's ugly head
All my enterprises soon dead
Hard work and sacrifice now gone
As many times before, on and on

Not once more, never again I'll fail
Beyond this life I will happily sail
My sick soul on I cannot force
I accept my end, and return to the source

Dolorous Mope

Why do I bother having friends?
They rarely seem to suit my ends
Talking with them brings anxiety much
Thus for me substantial pain as such

Oh there are those good times, sure
That occasionally my ills do cure
But these are so terribly rare
It is so difficult for me to care

If only friendship could be pure joy
I'd be so pleasant, cheerful, and cloy
Alas such blessings are not for me
Ever a dolorous mope I'll be

Dolorous Mope

Model: Makayla Niemier
IG: Pastel Punk Pirate

I am less

It is they whom you bless
The ones with low stress
Whose lives are not a mess
I am less

There are those who insult
They only cause tumult
Misery is their sole result
I am less

There are those who are whole
Possessed of a happy soul
Joy flows from their bowl
I am less

There is he who is strong
His heart full of song
With his friends does he belong
I am less

There is she who is alighted
With life she is delighted
Of dangers she is not afrighted
I am less

There are those who are alive
For accomplishments they strive
Busily building life's hive
I am less

There are those who with angst struggle
With dolor do they snuggle
Without magic like a muggle
I am less

There are those who have rights
Protections kept in their sights
For them another fights
I am less

In present pain I do toil
Ever my happiness does it spoil
Until I am buried in the soil
I am less

Incomplete

I am not quite alive
I simply did not die
I am what remained
The shell of what was once
A whole person
I am not real
Incomplete

The Despoiler

The despoiler strikes with spite
A great conflagration to incite
Launching weapons of mass destruction
My happiness in quick deconstruction

Complications in my friendships
My stock in life rapidly slips
Mushroom clouds over my treasures
The ruination of my few pleasures

Devastation in my life's courses
Bucked and thrown from my horses
Cursed like the Spanish Armada
A devil haunts me in her Prada

Stealing all my precious gold
All the winning cards does he hold
I am defenseless to his machinations
Dark, cold, and anxious sensations

Why am I his eternal victim?
Ever prey to his vile dictum
Who can this vindictive villain be?
With great irony I admit, he is me

Torturous Illness

Anxiety haunts my every breath
Living is such intense agony
My body filled with pain
My mind with anguish

This torpor hangs over me
It tears away my feelings
Distances me from love
Drowns my hope for the future

Under such torture why do I not die?
Why does my body endure this torment?
Just so I can suffer on another day
Misery awaiting my every awakening

Oh how I want freedom from this illness
What could life be if cured of the terminal?
No more self-loathing and insecurity
My dastardly misery finally ended

How I might revel in such euphoria!
I could love with passion
Be caring and compassionate
I would be kind and humble

A real person I would be
Like the others around me
Happy, sad, in love, or angry
But full of life and verve

The caress of my lover's neck
A hug for a friend in need
A reassuring word to the uncertain
Wisdom for the young

Alas, such occasions of health are rare
I fear the impending return of illness
I know only death's frigid kiss
Can truly rid me of my ailment

I soldier on in this cruel life
My works as yet incomplete
I try not to be undone by the disease
I neither surrender nor succumb

Let Go

Why do you make me stay around?
I could go sink into the ground
Life is disappointment and pain
Barely worth the effort; to what gain?

I could fly from here and cease to be
Why must this despair consume me
I cling to rare moments of pleasure

Few and infrequent that is sure
Let me go into the abstract ether
I can escape my tormentor, my beater
I'll find release in the nothing's finality

Free'd from the chains of dolorous mortality
How long must I wait this pain to be rid?
My loving heart buried deep and truly hid
I will try to believe my callous heart speak

Only more suffering as reward for a freak
I want to find a some meager way to cope
Once again to hold out for alluring hope
What shall I have for my naive faith?

More sadness shall haunt me as a wraith
To those young and full of life
Beware that great coming strife
"Carpe diem" the pleasures now before
In time your hope is crush'd forever more

Desolation

Courtesy Licensable

Emptiness

Oh how the onset of depression I despise
Visions of my death right behind my eyes
At the end of Anxiety's long road
Comes inevitably this life mode

Down, down, down I go into depths murky
That see me become the antonym of perky
Pain so great gives way to numbness
My brain now obsessed with dumbness

Feelings that were far away now gone
Love, sadness, anger, will not spawn
I am but a shell of a living being
Dead in every way but in other's seeing

I am not a real person, now only a husk
Waking with difficulty just before dusk
Going down in the twilight of dawn
To my disease, I am but a pawn

Dreadful emptiness fills my heart
From this reality I may as well part
How little my death would differ
From the current state, albeit stiffer

I'll wander on in the dark caverns alone
No other can join me in this null zone
Months of pain this basin to reach
For its end I so beg and beseech

Emptiness

Courtesy Licensable

Anxious Anger

My body prepares for a fight to the death
Blood pressure rises, I've lost my breath
I am under attack once again
Suffering this incredible pain

My senses become hyper aware
I look for any threat that might dare
My skin burns, my breath short
Yet there is no danger of great import

References to torments long passed
Many times was I abused and harassed
At a moment's notice it rises anew
My mood and thoughts torn askew

Evil people live rent free in my head
Sometimes I think I'd be better off dead
So I don't have to experience this misery
Destruction of my body with mental artillery

Why cannot I not let go of this suffering?
That causes my mind lengthy buffering
My choices now are entirely undesirable
This anxious pain and depression miserable

Or days of tears and angst, weakness terrible
Vulnerable emotions: hurt and injury ineffable
Or no feeling at all: depression, undead
Hours wasted without motivation in bed

I want freedom from this unending cycle
My feelings trapped in an endless epicycle
I do not know how to escape this horror
As my soul grows weaker and pourer

I want to hate they who caused my ire
Their destruction my sole desire
What would that solve to be so cruel?
My decency gone as the blood would pool

Evil for evil will bring me no justice
Causing pain brings no solace
So I suffer alone and secluded
My humanity crushed and extruded

My mind turns to my own destruction
My body's physical deconstruction
I could hit, smash, bruise, and inflict
Upon myself the injury of this conflict

To resist the urge is extremely difficult
As the intensity of anxiety does catapult
Why is it I who must suffer so?
From the words of scum, I barely know

It is, I suppose my life's great curse
The masochistic tango, I rehearse
For now, my life does tear and bend
Hashem please bring this torture to an end

To Heal What I Feel

If I cut my flesh it will quickly heal
Blood will flow and quickly seal
But the hurt inside is what I feel
What I feel I cannot seal or heal

This is my struggle, my strife
From the beginning of life
On the cutting edge of the knife
Can the knife end my life and strife?

Perhaps my heart can retrain
My life I can try to sustain
To end this self-disdain
No more disdain, I can sustain and retrain

I never feel good enough
I am weak, not strong or tough
I do not have the right stuff
The stuff to be tough enough

I seek the peace of the dove
In the power of true love
This pain I can rise above
Above with love like the dove

Memphis Night

Isaac Kight Original Art

Better than Suicide

A few happy moments break the dolor
I cannot find contentment in its color
Struggling on to earn a dollar
To my illness a slave with a collar

So much pain and misery abound
A depressing and negative sound
At high anxiety my heart does pound
Not for long is any peace found

Oh how I desire an expedient escape
In scarlet streams my body to drape
Or a wound at my neck's nape
Never more to unwind life's tape

Instead I choose to suffer on
Much injury heaped upon
Promise cut off short like a lawn
At times I nearly died at life's dawn

But that path would be too quick
An easy end would be so slick
In seconds away my pain would tick
Back to life's source I would pick

So I go on in misery and sorrow
No relief awaits upon the marrow
Perhaps some pleasure I might barrow?
It is but fleeting, takes flight as a sparrow

Is it possible I deserve better?
To this illness I am a debtor
I cannot imagine being absent this letter
I feel I deserve this suffering, a fetter

These torments I cannot abide
From the torture I cannot hide
I think of death, I must confide
This suffering is better than suicide

A Cry for Release

Oh callous death, would you call my name?
End this dolorous life if it's just the same
It is not I who is for this tragedy to blame
Terrible illness of my soul I could not tame

I began life and so soon was I cast away
Over my circumstances I had no say
Never of my volition would it be this way
I suffer intensely each and every day

I have failed everyone especially those I love
This incapacity I cannot rise above
A cancer of my sanity that I am dying of
Make a quick end, just the slightest shove

I am mused with such eloquent creativity
Without limit, ineffable, beyond relativity
And yet it seems so vaporous of vanity
I feel so useless in my taciturn insanity

I wish an end to this terrific torment
There is a solution so entirely permanent
Yet only more suffering would this cement
For those who are wholly upon me dependent

It is they I must ultimately fail
As against this illness I fight and flail
Oh sweet death with you I could sail
Make this useless body morbidly pale

Why is there no answer to my cry?
Has your compassion run dry?
From this life I so wish to fly
Grant me redress that I may die

Unblemished

Isaac Kight Original Art

Existential Crisis

The existentialists say
Life is miserable anyway
Once you acknowledge the fact
You can choose to how act

Two choices then do confront
Both to G-d an affront
In utter misery to live
Or to end life, not to forgive

I can live in this lie
Or choose to die
I can run and hide
But I cannot confide

Life for me is torture
I am too immature
Why do I choose this?
The end I dismiss

Must I live on in dolor?
Constant pain in my molar
Injured in my heart
Right at life's start

This must not be me
Somewhere else I'm free
Living a happy way
Bright and sunny day

No this curse is my reality
Free from it I'll never be
Until death does liberate
From existence that does not sate

For reasons to me unknown
I keep going on my own
Nurturing the seeds sown
Until they are fully grown

The End I Know is Nigh

My mind is ailing
My marriage is failing
I am falling from the sky

My body so hurts
As my mind flirts
With the end I know to be nigh

The hour is numb
The time has come
I can hear time ticking by

While I can still feel
Was this world real?
Through time and space I fly

This great loss
Gave me a toss
This life I gave a try

I'll ignore my fears
Through all my tears
As the end I now spy

Through it all
My heart does call
For the one I now defy

When at my leisure
She was my pleasure
All I can do is cry

It could have been worse
Life is so terse
At my sanity it did pry

Now in this autumn
I've reached the bottom
I shed this life and die

The Anxiety Cycle

Down, down, low, low
Once more down the rabbit hole I go
My head and palms begin to sweat
I'm certain my stomach will soon be upset

My mind is fried, frazzled, and frail
Great intellect and creativity now set sail
I am once more just a dunce
Running scared, in crisis this once

Emotional pain wells up from inside
I cannot fight back or turn the tide
Soon meaningless tears will begin to fall
So many times I have gone through this all

Negative thoughts ride the wave
My mellow mood I cannot save
I think of all the worst times
When others attacked me, their crimes

Blood thickens, arteries grow tight
As my body prepares for the fight
Though no threat in truth exists
I am ready to fight death as it persists

Deeper, down, and deeper still
I go into my own hell against my will
Anger slowly starts to rise
My mind thinks it protects, just lies

How often the world sends me to this spiral?
To a terrible suffering too intensely viral
Unknown to those who trigger
As my torture grows ever bigger

How long does this go on?
So many torments to spawn
Hours, a day, three days on occasion
It answers to no control or persuasion

I cannot tell others of my plight
Too weak I'd seem, a victim in sight
So few understand what this does to me
How it weakens my very will to be

How could they know what they have done?
I cannot tell anyone who lives under the Sun
This cycle does end after time goes by
Yet, as I live through it I wish only to die

Birch Grove

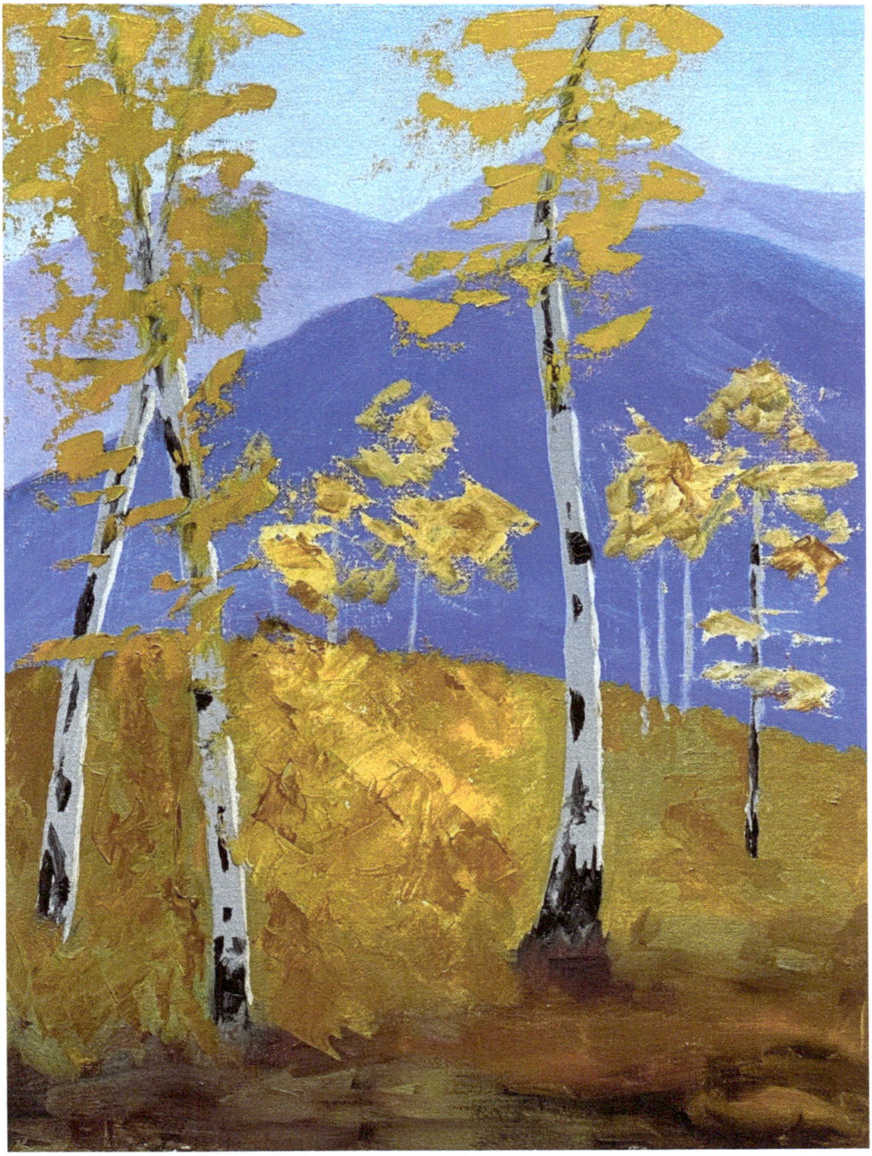

Painted by JP Forget

It's Okay

It is okay to mistreat me
I am not a real person
I died long ago
Only a shell remains
It is okay to judge me
To laugh when I have anxiety
To dismiss my struggles
To ignore my pleas for help
It is okay to insult me
The dead have no rights
I exist to be abused by others
Make the cut as deep as you like
It is okay to hurt me
Only real people have feelings
Mine do not matter
I am kicked when down
It is okay to exclude me
It is not as if I chose to be
I would not exist by choice
I am too difficult to bother with
It is okay to attack me
I am defenseless
There is little I can do
I do not fit the norm so I suffer
It is okay to hate me
I am too much trouble

I am the ultimate pariah
I am incapable of being loved
Is it okay...?
Can I just fade away...?

Family Curse

Family to me is so great a curse
As one is carried off in a hearse
The family politics are so terse
Everyone fighting for their purse

Years ago tragedy took us astray
Taking us from decency that day
Visiting evils on us, we had no say
Family tradition turned to clay

Abuse, a lack of love and nurturing
Ever impaired our efforts at maturing
Eternally to our anxiety catering
Our worst impulses we were flattering

The curse I have so long fought
To this effort I've given every thought
As to heal my pain I have sought
A better direction my children I have taught

The legacy going forward is the best
To end the insufferable abuse fest
To rise above unlike the rest
To live life with moral zest

In mourning now, I must be
Until happier days I will see
To a righteous life I can flee
From this pain I wish to be free

Frigid Wood

Isaac Kight Original Art

Constant Cruelty

The pain of life grown more intense
As frequent pangs it does dispense
Physical pain would be bearable
If mental anguish were not as terrible

This life has been an abject failure
I have nothing left, no savior
Perhaps I should let go of this form
So great a departure from the norm

Can I find peace beneath the soil?
By shedding the agony of this mortal coil
I do not know, I cannot say
So I suffer on yet another day

Buried in this unending self-loathing
Contemplating intense self-immolating
Why should I endure incredible pain?
So much suffering I cannot explain

Everyone feels at liberty to disparage me
I am not a real person, though I want to be
I have no rights, no feelings to respect
I died long ago in truth, as I reflect

I am a great pariah it is little wonder
As all my dreams have been torn asunder
With others I cannot positively relate
Their demands of me I am unable to sate

This life is but interminable waste
I should bring it to a close with haste
I did not choose to be what I am now
Human cruelty upon me and how

As a child beaten and cast aside
My treatment by others I cannot abide
Cruelty is constant, it defines humanity
It drives us all toward collective insanity

So I am this monster I have been made
Society excludes me, socially stayed
How much longer will I resist?
As my agonies do persist

Terminally Mentally Ill

I have to carry such burdens I know
Ever present struggle with little to show
Life is pain and suffering, I am always ill
My heart could stop beating, it could be still

I did nothing wrong, why must I suffer?
Fighting just to live and earn our supper
It could all end so painlessly and quickly
This life I did not want, my mind so sickly

I can see the future in all its glory
My miseries multiply, they are so hoary
Nothing changes, I cannot heal
This life is fiction, it cannot be real

Why do I go on, when I could end it all?
The misery of my life I might forestall
There is no pleasure for me to feel
My every happy moment it does steal

For some reason I hold on to hope
Some small measure that helps me cope
Is it delusion, is my situation hopeless?
Perhaps it is, I continue under duress

This illness is killing me, day by day
In its inordinately slow, insidious way
I know I cannot win, eventually it will
Bring my end, I am terminally mentally ill

Seppuku

Art by Skelefrog via DeviantArt.com

ADIDA-cide

All Day I Dream About suicide
Terrible feelings, I cannot turn the tide
All the many ways I could meet my end
The terrors I feel, how can I defend?

I think of so many ways I could
The many times I feel I should
I could have leapt from a ship
Or from great height had a clever slip

A fall into water would mean drowning
Or perhaps some poison downing
A gun would be messy and quick
To Sallie's Plan I might stick

Auto accidents occur so often
Why never to me, my suffering to soften?
Oh to fall asleep one happy evening
Never again to experience eyes opening

Starvation and dehydration take too long
Exsanguination requires one to be strong
Far too often do I find myself in this place
Is the suffering not written upon my face?

So eager am I to bring close to this anguish
Even for my own death I do wish
How many tears have I cried?
As this these desires I have defied

My entire life it seems
I have had these day dreams
Even as a child I suffered this thought
That I by my own hand I might exist not

The Accomplice

I exist to be the target of others
Their daily onslaught smothers
Not a real person, not fully human
Any liberty is taken anyone can

I am the one it is okay to abuse
Ever have I been a toy to amuse
Everyone looks on watching the harm
No one bothers to raise any alarm

The world's whipping boy, I am
I live only so others can damn
They insult, hit, kick, and spit
I am allowed no defense I must take it

When I fight back I am in the wrong
I am punished for not playing along
I should be able to know my place
As they deride and spit in my face

Those I dared once to call friend
Stood by and watched abuse without end
At times it overwhelms, it is too much
I consider ending the cycle as such

Again and again I am abandoned with ease
Warmth of friendship so quickly can freeze
Many pretend to be kind immeasurable
Just to find a moment when I am vulnerable

That is when the next blow does fall
The injury done is honestly small
You cannot hurt what is not real
What pretends to live, cannot feel

I am not a real person you see
I have no rights to defend, not me
I died forty years ago, what's left is a shell
Locked in a cruel world, a living hell

Tormented day and night by mankind
Some small kindness never to find
Every indignity that they do hurl
Causes my atomic anger to unfurl

My chest white hot, my mind a blur
That is when acts of justice occur
I am finally free to uncoil and strike
Free to destroy the evil as I like

This is when I become their accomplice
I lose any semblance of my conscience
For the one they despise I hate all the more
The knife through my own skin will bore

It is the true pariah that must be destroyed
By any means that can be employed
The final judgement arrives and justice uncurls
Now I am become Death, the destroyer of worlds

Note: "Now I am become death, the destroyer of worlds" is from the Bhagavad-Gita (a Hindu scripture) and was quoted by Robert Oppenheimer upon the first successful test of the Atomic Bomb. The quote is used here as a clever euphemism for suicide.

Little Pleasure

Life is misery there is little pleasure
You will not find it in great measure
Some think life such a treasure
I wish it could end at my leisure

Heart Be Still

Through the glassy water I see her face
Something is wrong and out of place
Her loving expression had given way
To a terrible seriousness that day

Each day is a struggle against my illness
There is no cure until death in its stillness
I do not want to die or be killed
But I do not want to live, my heart be stilled

Too Much

This pain is too much to bear
The tightness in my chest is not fair
The burning in my gut so intense
The pain in my limbs I constantly sense

Of this pain I want to be free
It seems that an end can never be
Why can't this body just die already?
Why the pain and suffering so steady?

My mind thinks of creative ways to die
I cannot make it stop no reason why
There is nought precious in this existence
Yet to its end is there so much resistance

Why struggle so for the life I do not want?
My pains and traumas do ever taunt
Why does this misery go on with malice?
It's end would bring peace and justice

I strike myself to feel the sting
The pain is calming, comforting
Why must I hurt myself so?
Why will this suffering not go?

In this very season did it nearly end
A child about two could not fend
A mothers love suddenly come to wrath
As she nearly drowned me in a bath

Why couldn't she but finish the deed?
Spare me this suffering and need?
A life of terrible struggle and grief
My hope, love of life lost to the thief

It seems pointless to perseverate
My suffering it does not mitigate
What shall be my ultimate plight?
To die young or for life to fight?

If I could make my mind to quiet
No more on suicidal thoughts to diet
I demand that it come to a stop
Before it boils over the top

I demand that I be made free
An end to this life for me
Or an end to the misery I feel
Is any of this even real?

One way or the other would be fine
The burden lifted off this heart of mine
I do not trust my feelings one bit
Too often they cast me into a fit

Everything about me is wrong and broken
There are those who tolerate me as a token
Everyone says I am a nut, crazy
My judgement opaque and hazy

I cannot live in this dour space
A happier complexion to replace
I feel so cold, so alone, forgotten

I should never have been begotten

It was wrong from the very start
From birth my life torn entirely apart
I tried my best to make do
I tried so hard to love you

I am not certain I truly feel anything
Feelings come and go a fleeting
I wanted to make it all right
But I lost my way, I lost my sight

Should I continue to try?
Is it all really just a lie?
The world so cold I feel nothing warm
My pains and angsts do swarm

It is time to let go of the charade
No longer this pathetic parade
The cold is comforting somehow
I can finally let go of everything now

The world will get on without me
This spectacle ended of insanity
Yet must I ever struggle with the plot
Ongoing suffering is my life's lot

I am broken, a failed life cast aside
But surrender to despair I cannot abide
Just short of a miserable death am I
On with the parody of my life I'll fly

Continental Divide

Isaac Kight Original Art

Toying

Why does life with me toy
Everything a trick or ploy
When I finally feel right
Disaster comes in sight

All my life I was the pariah
A beaten insulted false messiah
Now I look around and see
Among the few who are sane

Heat

All day the pounding drum beat
The anxiety intense I feel the heat
Panic lies behind every corner
I have lost hope, I am a mourner

Please G-d let me go to my end
This constant suffering to fend
It's all my fault I'll shoulder the blame
Just free me from my eternal shame

I live in a world where I am hated
Kicked, punched, knocked and berated
It is okay, everyone get your thrill
It is okay to torment the mentally ill

All my life have I suffered so
Only more suffering did they all sow
I am a pariah, I am not wanted
I am constantly beaten and taunted

It has been clear from the very start
In this society I have no part
I brought children into a world so hateful
Was it a mistake so utterly spiteful?

How can I protect them from evil at hand?
We will plant our feet and make our stand
It is our society so cruel and cold
Who shall be of their wickedness told

VI

Poems of Others

Robert Mason

Robert Mason, one of my wife's ancestors, was a Welsh immigrant to the United States in the late nineteenth century. A tailor by trade, he lived the first half of his life in the coal country of Wales and the second half making clothes in the heart of America's early steel industry in Ohio. He was a Welsh nationalist with a passion for the early labor movements in Victorian Britain.

He was also an amateur poet, writing poetry throughout his life that reflected his values and his love of Welsh mythology and history. In 1880, toward the end of his life, he self-published a collection of poetry on various topics, under the nom de plume Rob o' th' Mist.

This book he sent back Wales, in addition to distributing it locally in Ohio, and the many poems in it dedicated to his love of his homeland ultimately earned him a lengthy obituary in a Welsh journal when he passed a couple years later. The following are two poems from that book reproduced here.

Hope's First Bright Dreams

"I'll win immortal honours,"
The poet proudly said,
And fame's bright rays seemed flashing then,
Around the dreamer's head;
"My lays shall thrill the peasant
Upon the moorland lone,
And every note my harp gives forth
Shall reach the monarch's throne."

Thus said the youthful minstrel,
For hope had kiss'd his brow,
But where are all those glorious dreams
Of fame and honour now?
The critic's pen has banish'd,
Those visions bright and fair,
The blighting sneer has reached his heart,
And left the impress there.

The artist in his garret,
Where wealth had never been,
Oft gazed enraptured on the walls,
Where hung his glorious scene.
Bold crags were in the distance,
Tinged by the evening's glow,
And beautiful appear'd the charms
That graced the vale below.

The world may shower its honours
On those whom fortune owns,
And life may throw its charms around
The occupants of thrones:
He hoped, that youthful artist,
To boast a prouder name;
Some jealous rival's censure mocked
Those brilliant hopes of fame.

Scorn not the faint notes, blending
With those more right and free;
The youthful bard, in future years,
Another Burns may be.
Chide not the aspirations
That fill the painter's breast,
Art's noble sons may hail him yet,
A monarch o'er the rest.

Not with the great and noble
Along does genius dwell,
She bids the toiling cotter's songs
The mighty anthem swell;
She seeks the lowly cottage,
Where oft the poet sings,
And soon the peasant boy can boast
A richer fame than kings.

Song of the Welsh Emigrant

Upon the steamer's deck I stand,
And strain my eyes in vain
Towards the lov'd romantic land
I ne'er may tread again.

Cambria! Thy crags no more I see
Such is the rhymer's fate;
I love the hill, the stream, the tree,
But tyranny I hate!

In mind, my little ones I see
Play on the village green:
May heaven guard each one and thee,
My own, my dear Kathleen!

Haste! Guardian angels, stretch thy wings
O'er mountain, lake, and main;
Oh! Save and guide those guileless ones
Safe to my arms again.

'Tis Freedom's home for those I seek,
Beyond the western wave;
The rustic bard must cross the deep
To find a freeman's grave;
Where the artizan is deemed a man,
Nor treated as a slave.

"Class legislation" -- sable bane!
Darkens my native land,
Causing her voiceless slaves to find
Homes on a foreign strand.

The bold "Milesian" plows the deep
And "Albion's" noble land,
On from Silurian plain and steep
Go men of iron hand!

'Twas ever thus we tread the track
The "Pilgrim Fathers trod:"
Free homes we seek, and what sought they,
"Freedom to worship God!"

In a tiny grave by Vaga's stream
My gold-hair'd girl, with moans
I leave–my mother's ashes and
My honour'd father's bones.

My sainted Annie's dear remains
Rests in a quiet grave–
Which I, alas! No more may see–
By Ebbw's darken'd wave.

Why force us from our native land?
Are there not miles of soil,
Where rushes, gorse and thistles grow,
Would pay expense and toil?

The upland slope and moorland fens
Would grow the golden grain,
Should landlords give encouragement
To cultivate and drain.

The Cambrian thinks it hard to leave
His land of "harp and song;"
Necessity compels us,
But love of home is strong.

"Farewell to cataract, fair glen,
And native mountain side;
The sacred shrines and battle fields
Where heroes fought and died!

Wales is a semi-wilderness!
But still her sons–the best–
Are glad to seek the forests
And prairies of the West!

'Tis well! We'll lift our voices
Like the pilgrim sires of yore,
Who made their hallelujahs ring
On the free New England shore.

Nicole Reed

Lost in Fear

They always ask, "Why do you fight?"
I'm not fighting, I'm trying to explain
I'm not there but I'm not here
I'm stuck in some state of fear
I still don't know where I am
I'm lost and can't find my way
There are twists and turns in this tunnel
That I can't see ahead of me
Because it's dark
I have no light to guide me
I want you to know that I want out of this
Mess, but I don't even know what this is
I'm trying to understand why I am this way
But maybe...maybe this is me
Can't you see? I'm in a box with no escape
I bang on the walls with no sound
Where am I? Can anyone hear me?
I scream and cry but I still don't know why
I'm here
I can't leave, I can't
And I'm sorry.

About the Author

Isaac Kight

About the Author

Isaac Kight published Dark Recesses of the Mind: An Exploration of Depression, PTSD, and Poetic Forms in 2021. Writing poetry has been an important part of his self-expression during the process of treatment and recovery. As his poetry gained popularity on social media platforms the call rose for Isaac to publish his first book. With many new poems since that time on varied topics, he decided to publish a second book of poetry in this volume.

Isaac lives in the Midwest United States with his wife Rachel and their six children. He also publishes several popular shows and podcasts including Talking About Trauma, which discusses life with severe PTSD and the healing process. Isaac Kight is a transportation safety consultant, helping to ensure the safe movement of oversize truck loads ranging from space capsules and satellites, to natural gas infrastructure and wind turbine components.

Printed in the USA
CPSIA information can be obtained
at www.ICGtesting.com
LVHW020744051023
760085LV00053B/1084

9 798891 451728